WATCH THI GROW!

This book belongs to:

Animals in the book

WATCH THEM GROW!

Animal Life Cycles

James Carter and James Munro

GRAFFEG

Caterpillars
kittens, cubs
ducklings, pufflings
piglets, pups

Little creatures
all brand new
little lives
with much to do

Gaining strength
and gaining sight
gaining weight
and gaining height

Getting ready
for the time
they can swim
or sprint or fly

To the world now
we will go
turn the page and...

WATCH THEM GROW!

EMPEROR DRAGONFLY

Summertime
and days are long
in the weeds
around the pond

Little nymphs
are hatching here
live in water
for a year

Climbing reeds
and shedding skins
now whizzing off
with shiny wings

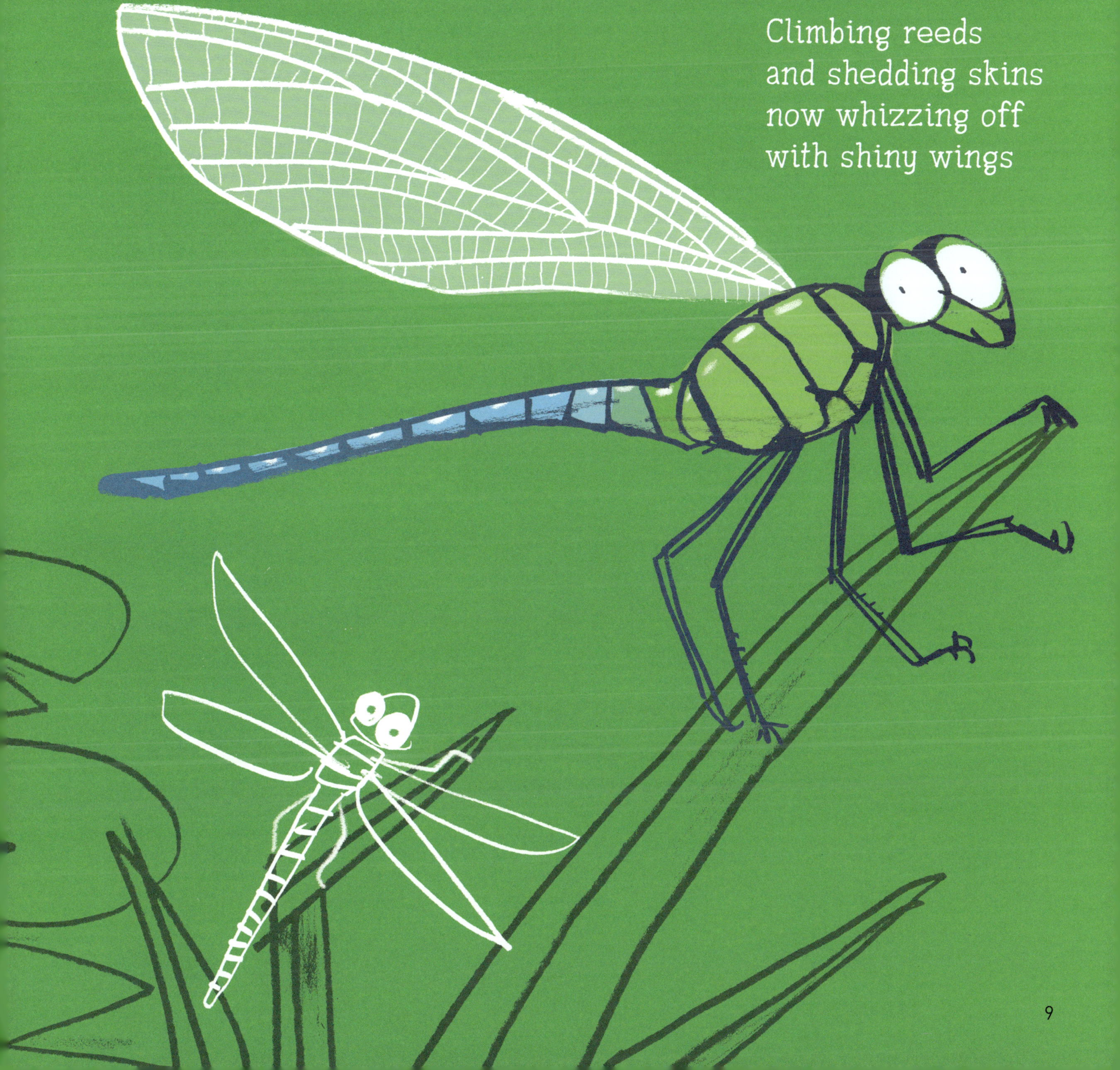

ANGLE SHADES MOTH

Out of eggs
so round and small
caterpillars
creep and crawl

Feasting
till it's time to be
pupas dangling
from a tree

When each shell
is shaken off
out will burst
a flappy moth

COMMON SEAHORSE

If you ever
get the chance
watch a seahorse
mating dance

Colours shifting
sideways grooving
heads a-clicking
non-stop moving

Only creatures
on this earth
where males take
the eggs to birth

COMMON FROG

Spring's returned
so warm winds blow
in the pond there
down below

Dot-like eggs
that soon will be
tiny tadpoles
jiggling free

Sprouting limbs
and hopping lots
when they're mini
speckled frogs

STARLING

Little beaks
and little wings
ever-hungry
chirpy things

Sky-blue eggs
begin to crack
five new fledglings
start to hatch

Getting ready
day and night
for their future...

BURMESE PYTHON

Mother coils
around her nest
to protect
her clutch of eggs

Several weeks
she'll have to wait
so that they can
incubate

And then those
wriggly snakelets need
to slither off
for their first feed

GREY WOLF

One spring den
so snug and warm
four new precious
pups are born

Deaf and blind
and there they'll stay
feed for weeks
until the day

They'll emerge
into the light
to join the pack
to hunt and fight

BOTTLENOSE DOLPHIN

Mother dolphin
swimming free
one whole year
her pregnancy

Births her calf
in shallow sea
her life will change
immediately

For now she'll spend
a month awake
to feed her calf
and keep it safe

HUMAN

First a baby
next a toddler
then a walking
talking wonder

Clever child
and one so bright
every day
brings new
delights

Here's a human
oh so new
it's the marvel
that is

YOU!

WATCH THEM GROW!
Watch them Grow! is a fun, rhyming text exploring some of nature's unique life cycles, including frogs, starlings, moths, turtles and more.
GRAFFEG
WATCH THEM GROW!
Animal Life Cycles
James Carter and James Munro
GRAFFEG

Little creatures
far to go
best of luck now...

OFF YOU GO!

A CALF is a baby cow – as well as a whale, dolphin, giraffe, elephant, rhino and moose.

WHOSE BABIES ARE THESE?

A GOSLING is a baby goose.

A JOEY is a baby kangaroo, wallaby and koala.

An INFANT is a baby monkey.

An ELVER is a baby eel.

A LEVERET is a baby hare.

A NYMPH is a baby grasshopper, aphid and mayfly.

A PUP is a baby dog – and a bat, hamster, dolphin, seal and mouse.

A HATCHLING is a baby bird – and also a tadpole, newt, turtle and crocodile.

A CUB is a baby aardvark – and a lion, tiger, bear, fox and wolf.

CAN YOU GUESS THESE ONES?

Antling...? Owlet...? Puffling...? Spiderling...?

WHO KNEW?

An AXOLOTL never really becomes an adult. Unlike other amphibians - such as toads, frogs and newts - an axolotl keeps its gills to breathe underwater and does not grow lungs, so cannot ever venture onto land.

A male SEAHORSE is quite unique in the animal kingdom in that it gives birth to hundreds of babies called fries. The female seahorses transfer the eggs to the male and he keeps them in a 'brood pouch' until they are ready to hatch some four weeks later. With all other creatures in the world it is the female that does all the hard work of childbirth.

Male EMPEROR PENGUINS are dedicated dads too. They stay to look after the single egg whilst the female goes off to sea to seek food, often for up to two months. The male keeps the egg in a flap of skin between its feet, not only protecting but 'incubating' the egg, keeping it warm and helping the young to develop. The chick hatches and the female returns soon after this, bringing food and taking over the parenting duties whilst the father goes off to feed himself.

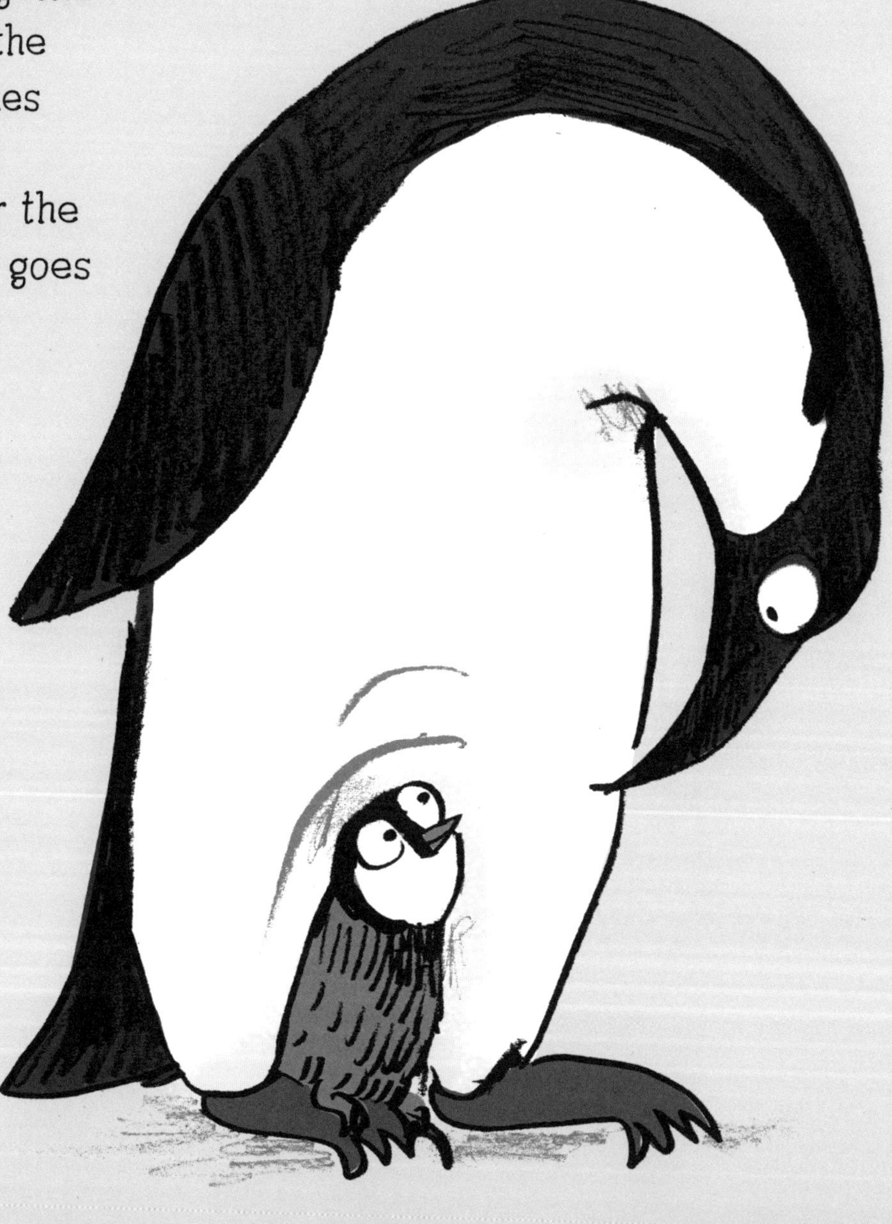

Australian marsupials - such as the KANGAROO, WALLABY, KOALA and WOMBAT - are the only creatures to keep their young in a mother's pouch. The young of these marsupials do not have long to develop. They are born weak and small so they are protected in these warm pockets until they have fed and grown and are ready to be more independent.

The most dedicated of all parents? A newborn DOLPHIN calf does not sleep for its first month, so the mother will stay awake that whole time to protect it. An ORANGUTAN cares for its young for eight years. HUMAN children nowadays stay at home until their late teens and early twenties!

Want to know a really fancy but very useful sciency word? METAMORPHOSIS. When applied to animals, it refers to the changes a creature goes through from birth to adulthood, as in the life cycles of a frog (egg – tadpole – adult frog) or a butterfly/moth (egg – caterpillar – pupa – adult butterfly).

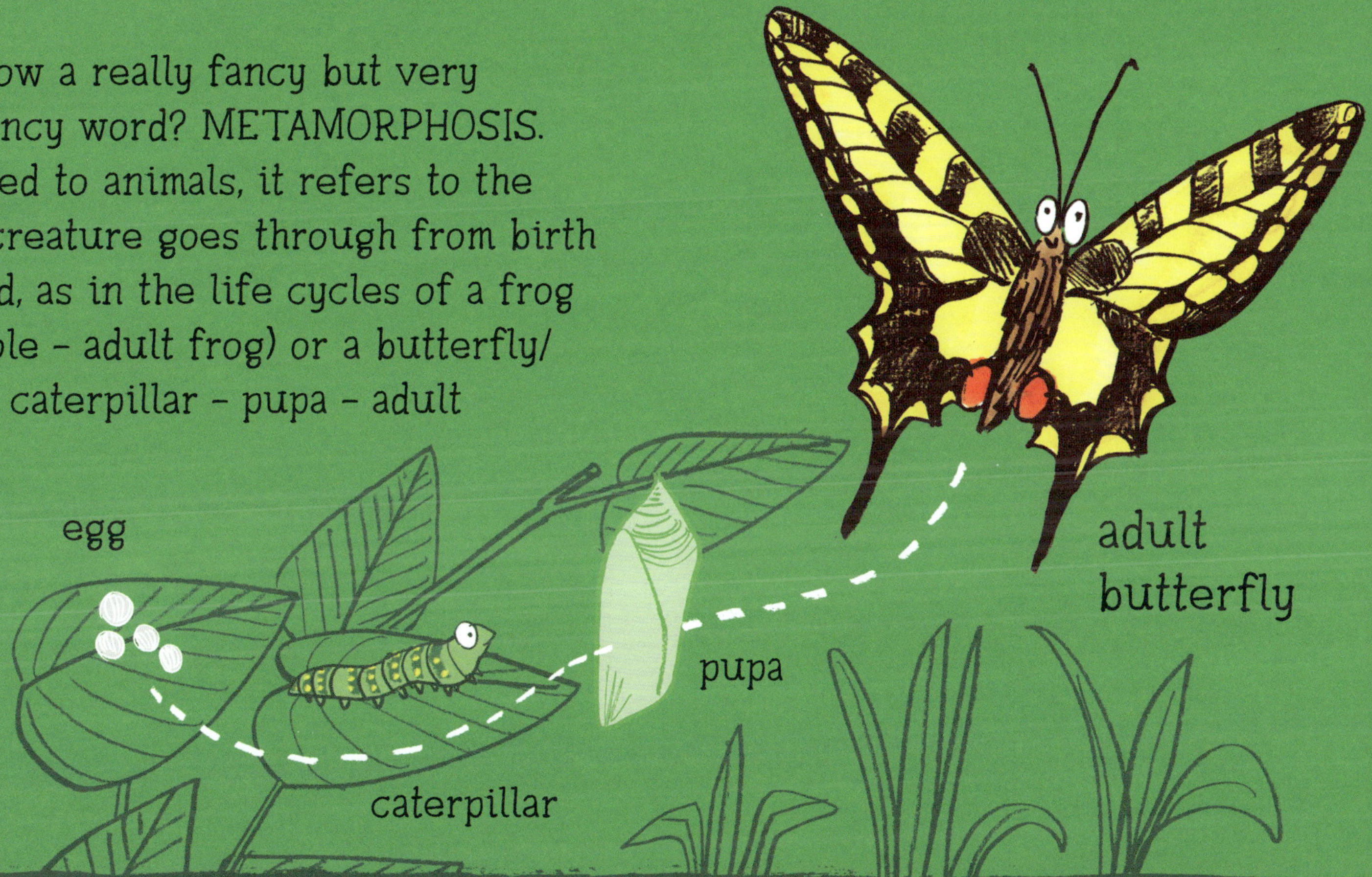

METAMORPHOSIS

For that brilliant organisation that does so much to keep the wild as wild as it can be - BBOWT - Berks Bucks & Oxon Wildlife Trust.
J.C.

For Toucan & Songbird - I have loved watching you fledglings learn to fly.
J.M.

Watch Them Grow!
Published in Great Britain in 2024 by Graffeg Limited.

Graffeg Limited, 24 Stradey Park Business Centre, Mwrwg Road, Llangennech, Llanelli, Carmarthenshire, SA14 8YP, Wales, UK.
Tel: 01554 824000. www.graffeg.com.

James Carter and James Munro are hereby identified as the author and the illustrator of this work in accordance with section 77 of the Copyright, Designs and Patents Act 1988.

A CIP Catalogue record for this book is available from the British Library.

ISBN 9781802586633

1 2 3 4 5 6 7 8 9

FSC www.fsc.org MIX Paper from responsible sources FSC® C014138